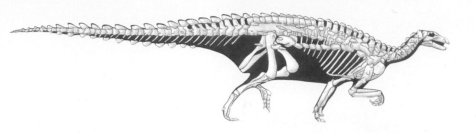

Awesome Dinosaurs
ARMORED GIANTS

Michael Benton

COPPER BEECH BOOKS
Brookfield, Connecticut

© Aladdin Books Ltd 2001

Produced by:
Aladdin Books Ltd
28 Percy Street
London W1P 0LD

ISBN 0–7613–2161–6

*First published in the United
States in 2001 by:*
Copper Beech Books,
an imprint of
The Millbrook Press
2 Old New Milford Road
Brookfield,
Connecticut 06804

Editor:
Kathy Gemmell

Designers:
Flick, Book Design & Graphics
Simon Morse

Illustrators:
James Field, Ross Watton—SGA
Additional illustrations:
Sarah Smith—SGA
Cartoons: Jo Moore

Certain illustrations have
appeared in earlier
books created by
Aladdin Books.

Printed in UAE
Cataloging-in-Publication data is
on file at the Library of Congress.

Contents

Introduction

Find out for yourself all about the dinosaurs with spikes and armor that roamed Earth millions and millions of years ago.

Dinosaurs were among the most successful animals of all time. They lived on Earth for many, many years. Scientists called paleontologists are constantly unearthing amazing information and making exciting new discoveries about armored dinosaurs and their world. They study remains, called fossils, which have been preserved in ancient rocks.

Spot and count!

Q: Why watch out for these boxes?

A: They give answers to the dinosaur questions you always wanted to ask.

zoom in on...

Dinosaur bits

Look out for these boxes to take a closer look at armored dinosaurs.

Awesome facts

Watch out for these diamonds to learn more about the truly weird and wonderful facts about armored dinosaurs and their world.

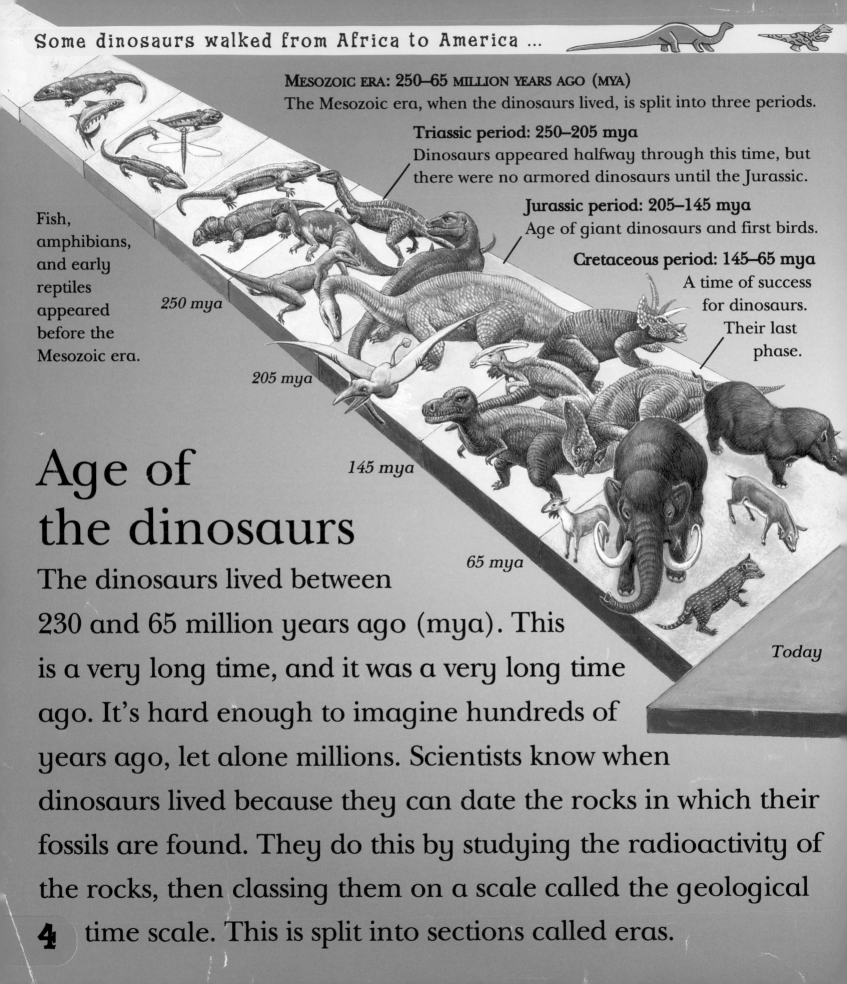

MESOZOIC ERA: 250–65 MILLION YEARS AGO (MYA)
The Mesozoic era, when the dinosaurs lived, is split into three periods.

Triassic period: 250–205 mya
Dinosaurs appeared halfway through this time, but there were no armored dinosaurs until the Jurassic.

Jurassic period: 205–145 mya
Age of giant dinosaurs and first birds.

Cretaceous period: 145–65 mya
A time of success for dinosaurs. Their last phase.

Fish, amphibians, and early reptiles appeared before the Mesozoic era.

250 mya

205 mya

145 mya

65 mya

Today

Age of the dinosaurs

The dinosaurs lived between 230 and 65 million years ago (mya). This is a very long time, and it was a very long time ago. It's hard enough to imagine hundreds of years ago, let alone millions. Scientists know when dinosaurs lived because they can date the rocks in which their fossils are found. They do this by studying the radioactivity of the rocks, then classing them on a scale called the geological time scale. This is split into sections called eras.

4

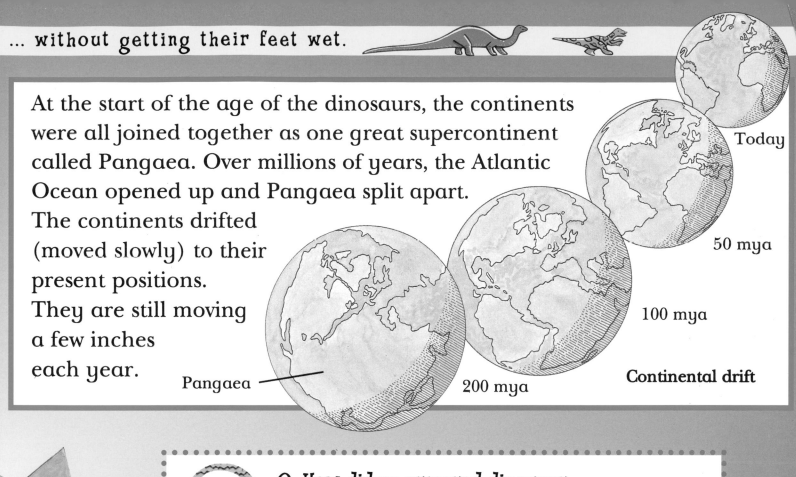

At the start of the age of the dinosaurs, the continents were all joined together as one great supercontinent called Pangaea. Over millions of years, the Atlantic Ocean opened up and Pangaea split apart. The continents drifted (moved slowly) to their present positions. They are still moving a few inches each year.

Today

50 mya

100 mya

Continental drift

Pangaea

200 mya

Q: How did an armored dinosaur become a fossil?

A: Small meat-eating animals ate the flesh from the dead dinosaur's bones. Some bones rotted. Others were buried under layers of sand or mud. These turned into fossils over time, as tiny spaces in the bones filled with rock. Millions of years later, the fossilized bones are uncovered by water or wind action. Paleontologists dig the fossilized bones out of the rock and clean them, making sure they don't fall apart. They make maps and take photographs at the dig site so that they can tell later exactly where everything was found.

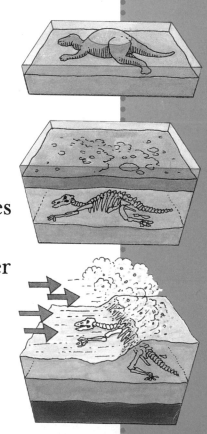

All kinds of armor

The armored dinosaurs, called the thyreophorans, lived through the Jurassic and Cretaceous periods. The stegosaurs were particularly important during the Late Jurassic and the ankylosaurs flourished during the Cretaceous.

Ankylosaurs, such as *Hylaeosaurus*, were covered in bony armor, and some had large spines along their sides. Stegosaurs, such as *Kentrosaurus*, had spines and plates down the middle of their back.

Hylaeosaurus

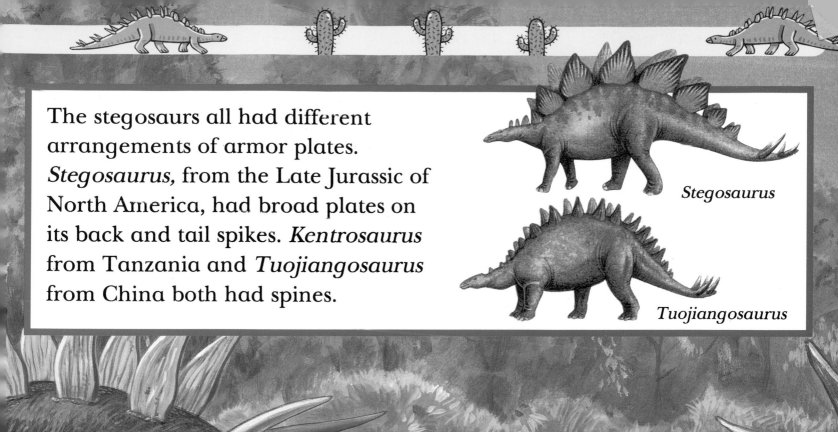

The stegosaurs all had different arrangements of armor plates. *Stegosaurus,* from the Late Jurassic of North America, had broad plates on its back and tail spikes. *Kentrosaurus* from Tanzania and *Tuojiangosaurus* from China both had spines.

Stegosaurus

Tuojiangosaurus

Kentrosaurus

Plates on end

The most famous stegosaur, *Stegosaurus*, had broad, flat plates down its back. People once thought they lay flat to form a kind of shell, but markings at the base of the plates show that they stood upright. What were they for?

zoom in on...

Small brains

Stegosaurus is known as the most stupid dinosaur. It had a brain the size of a walnut. There was actually a second "brain" in the hip region, which operated the hind legs and tail.

Second "brain"

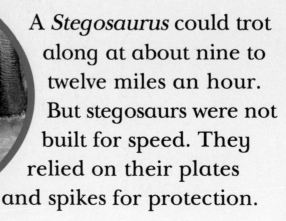

A *Stegosaurus* could trot along at about nine to twelve miles an hour. But stegosaurs were not built for speed. They relied on their plates and spikes for protection.

8

The plates on *Stegosaurus* were for protection and temperature control. Fossils show that they were covered with skin and had large blood vessels. When *Stegosaurus* was angry or hot, it pumped blood over the plates. This made them flush red and also shed heat.

Blood vessels

9

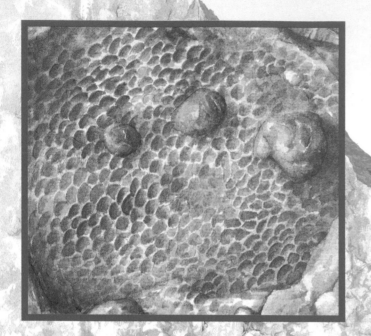

A recent specimen of *Scelidosaurus*, on display at the Bristol City Museum in England, shows excellent detail of the skull. Some of the skin has even been preserved. The pattern on the skin shows a kind of chain mail of tiny bony plates all over it.

Scelidosaurus was a sleek animal, about thirteen feet long. It trotted around on all fours, seeking ferns and other low plants. Scientists know that it evolved from a two-legged ancestor, since the hind legs are much longer than the front legs. There were seven main rows of bony spines running the length of the body.

Spot two other *Scelidosaurus*.

Early trotters

The first armored dinosaur was from the Early Jurassic of southern England. Called *Scelidosaurus*, paleontologists have debated for years whether it is a stegosaur or an ankylosaur—it seems to have been ancestor to both groups.

Scelidosaurus nipped off leaves, then pulled them back into its mouth with its tongue. The cheek pouches saved it from losing bits of food out of the sides.

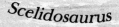

Scelidosaurus

zoom in on...

Complete skeleton

Scelidosaurus was the first complete dinosaur skeleton and one of the first armored forms ever discovered. It was named in 1860 by Sir Richard Owen.

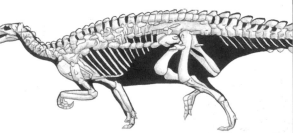

Monster museum

Many dinosaurs have been found in China since 1970. One of the most spectacular sites is the Dashanpu Quarry at Zigong in Sichuan province, where a group of dinosaurs from the Middle Jurassic has been unearthed. A key discovery was the stegosaur *Tuojiangosaurus*, of which twelve skeletons exist.

Tuojiangosaurus

12

The Zigong site was discovered by Dong Zhiming, a leading Chinese paleontologist based in Beijing. He has named many amazing new dinosaurs.

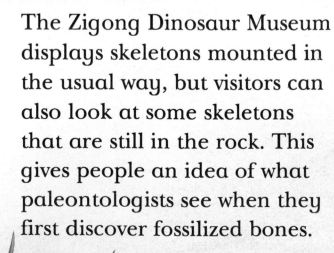

The Zigong Dinosaur Museum displays skeletons mounted in the usual way, but visitors can also look at some skeletons that are still in the rock. This gives people an idea of what paleontologists see when they first discover fossilized bones.

Kentrosaurus, from the Late Jurassic of Tanzania in Africa, may have been able to rear up and snatch leaves from low levels in trees. Giant plant eaters, such as *Barosaurus* and *Brachiosaurus*, fed at higher levels.

Kentrosaurus

zoom in on...

Stegosaur teeth

Stegosaurs had long, narrow jaws and teeth that were quite short. The jaws were not built for chomping twigs and tough plant food, nor were the teeth—the teeth had a shaped edge that was very useful for cutting leaves.

Leaf eaters

Stegosaurs were plant eaters. They fed on low bushes and trees, tearing out leaves and chomping them. However, they mostly ate soft leaves, since their teeth were not very powerful.

Stegosaurs probably ate ferns and seed ferns close to the ground, and the lower leaves of conifer trees, such as the monkey puzzle. There were no deciduous trees or flowering plants in the Late Jurassic.

Gasosaurus

Squaring up

It seems certain that armored dinosaurs used their armor to stand up to predators. *Huayangosaurus*, a stegosaur from the Middle Jurassic of China, could face up to the meat eater *Gasosaurus* just by looking scary.

Stegosaurs might have used their sharp spines to square up to rivals as well. The bigger one probably scared the smaller one away.

Huayangosaurus

Q: What could a stegosaur do with its tail?

A: Whack its enemies! There were powerful muscles in the tail, and it could deliver a wounding blow. A meat eater could get a slash up to three feet long in its flesh. No thanks!

Stegosaurs were mostly placid animals, but an attacker would face a furious defense—red-flushing spines and plates, and a wickedly spiked, swiping tail.

17

zoom in on...

Thick legs

Ankylosaurs had short, fat legs with unusually broad and short bones. The bones had to be stout to support the great weight of all the armor.

Hylaeosaurus

Polacanthus and *Hylaeosaurus* lived in mixed herds in the Early Cretaceous of southern England. These two dinosaurs were very similar, except that they had different patterns on their armor.

Walking works

The ankylosaurs were slow movers and were smaller than the stegosaurs. They didn't have to move fast—with a heavy armor of plates all over their body, they were safe from attackers. Even if it wanted to, an ankylosaur couldn't shift all that weight at any faster than a stroll.

Polacanthus

Fossilized tracks show that ankylosaurs moved slowly. The footprints are spaced close together, suggesting that the maximum speed they could reach was perhaps six miles per hour—the same speed you go when you jog. You could easily beat one in a sprint race!

Flower chompers

The ankylosaurs lived mainly in lowland areas near lakes and rivers. They fed on lush plants around these watery habitats, but could not reach up high into trees or go up on their hind legs.

How many different kinds of flowers?

 Q: Why did some ankylosaurs have broader mouths than others?

A: The shape of their mouths tells us about the food they ate. A broad mouth, like *Sauropelta*'s, means it cropped all kinds of plants and flowers. A narrow mouth, like *Polacanthus*'s, means it probably only ate certain plants.

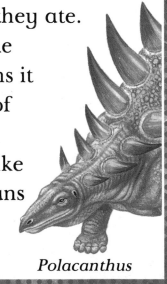

Polacanthus

20

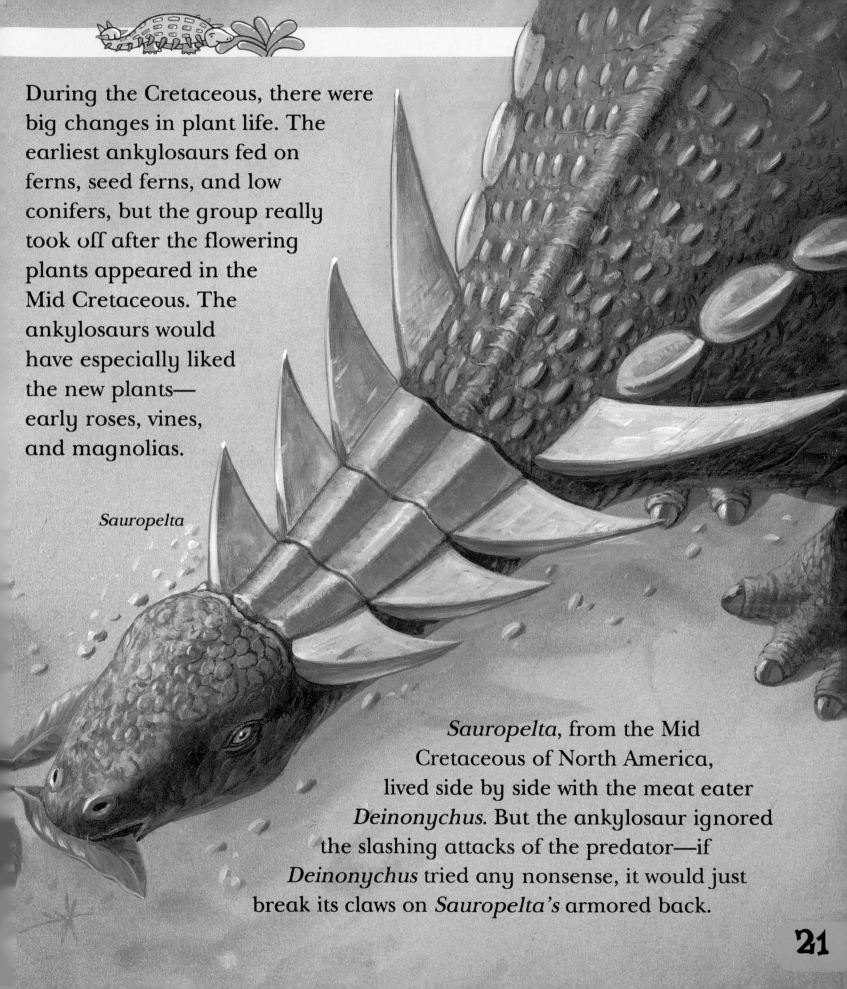

During the Cretaceous, there were big changes in plant life. The earliest ankylosaurs fed on ferns, seed ferns, and low conifers, but the group really took off after the flowering plants appeared in the Mid Cretaceous. The ankylosaurs would have especially liked the new plants— early roses, vines, and magnolias.

Sauropelta

Sauropelta, from the Mid Cretaceous of North America, lived side by side with the meat eater *Deinonychus*. But the ankylosaur ignored the slashing attacks of the predator—if *Deinonychus* tried any nonsense, it would just break its claws on *Sauropelta's* armored back.

21

Baby snatchers

One of the scariest ankylosaurs was *Edmontonia*. Powerful and sturdy, this ankylosaur also sprouted great spines along its sides. It was about twenty feet long, and weighed up to eleven tons. Attackers would think twice before tackling such a monster!

A baby *Edmontonia* may have seemed a tasty meal for a meat eater, but the parents would soon scare it off.

Edmontonia

Awesome facts

Two specimens of *Edmontonia* were mummified—dried out by the heat—and they show how the spikes were arranged.

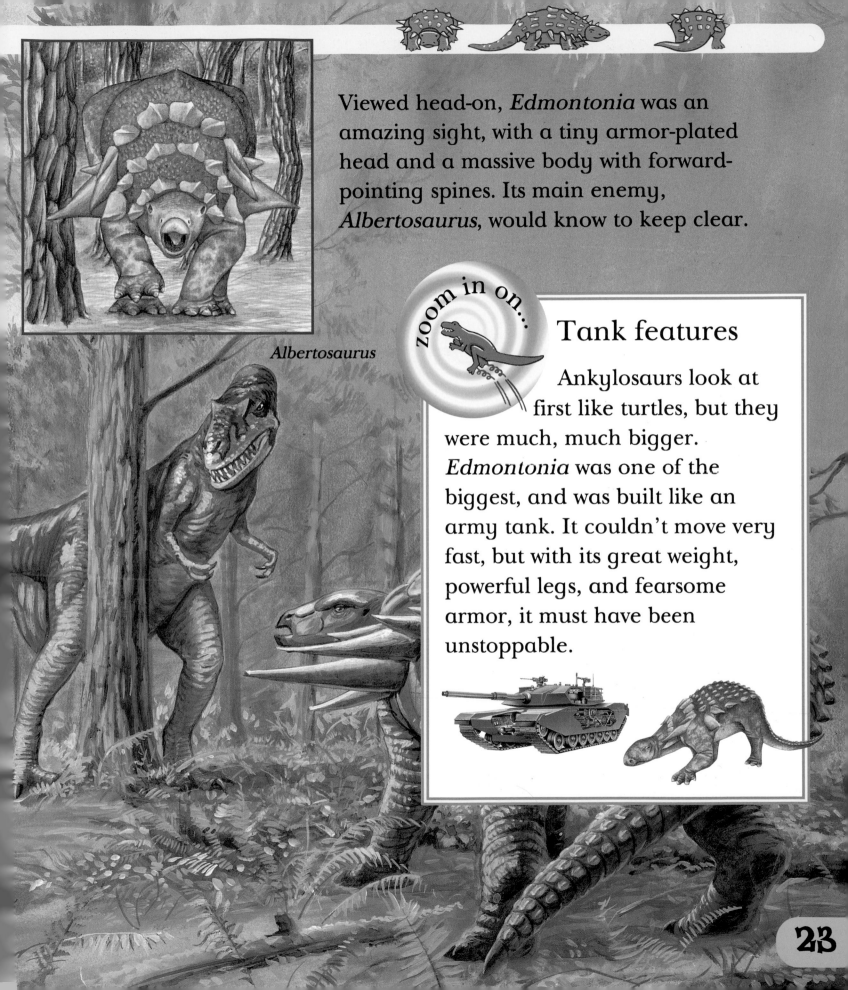

Viewed head-on, *Edmontonia* was an amazing sight, with a tiny armor-plated head and a massive body with forward-pointing spines. Its main enemy, *Albertosaurus*, would know to keep clear.

Albertosaurus

zoom in on...

Tank features

Ankylosaurs look at first like turtles, but they were much, much bigger. *Edmontonia* was one of the biggest, and was built like an army tank. It couldn't move very fast, but with its great weight, powerful legs, and fearsome armor, it must have been unstoppable.

Ankylosaurs had a special pattern of armor plates over their heads. There was a second layer of bones over the normal skull bones. The armor plating even extended to special bony ridges over the nostrils and a bony eyelid cover. No predator could possibly bite through all that!

Boned up

Ankylosaurs were the best protected animals of all time. Even the head had its own special armor plating. *Talarurus*, of the Late Cretaceous of Mongolia, is a typical ankylosaur. It was protected from its predators by armor, bony spines, and a bony ball on the end of its tail.

How many *Talarurus* can you spot?

Talarurus

Q: Did *Talarurus* have more bones than other dinosaurs?

A: A typical dinosaur had about 350 bones in its skull and skeleton. Ankylosaurs like *Talarurus* had far more—their armor could add about three hundred major bony plates and spines along the back, plus fifty or so extra bone plates around the head, and hundreds of small bone plates in the skin. Humans have only about 250 bones.

Awesome factS

Ankylosaurs had so much armor that the skeleton and armor together could make up more than half their total body weight.

Fighting

Ankylosaur armor was for defense, but also for fighting. Male ankylosaurs probably fought their predators and each other. Unlike *Hylaeosaurus* and *Sauropelta,* with their straight tails, *Talarurus* and *Euoplocephalus* had bony tail clubs to fight with.

zoom in on...

Bony tail

The tail club was made from the last three or four vertebrae in the tail, fused into a hard, bony blob. It was heavy and could very easily knock out a predator.

Euoplocephalus

Male ankylosaurs probably fought rivals by posing and roaring. The smaller one would eventually be scared off. If the two were equally matched, they might barge into each other, whacking with their tails. But the armor would protect them from serious injury.

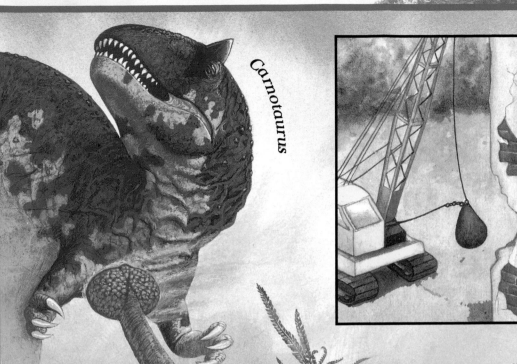

Carnotaurus

The tail club was like a steel wrecking ball used to demolish walls. Ankylosaurs could kill predators with their tail clubs if they hit them hard enough in the right place.

Euoplocephalus, from the Late Cretaceous of North America, lived at the same time as the meat eater *Carnotaurus.* They must have faced each other often, but after it had been whacked about a bit, *Carnotaurus* would probably have learned not to tackle the ankylosaur.

Euoplocephalus

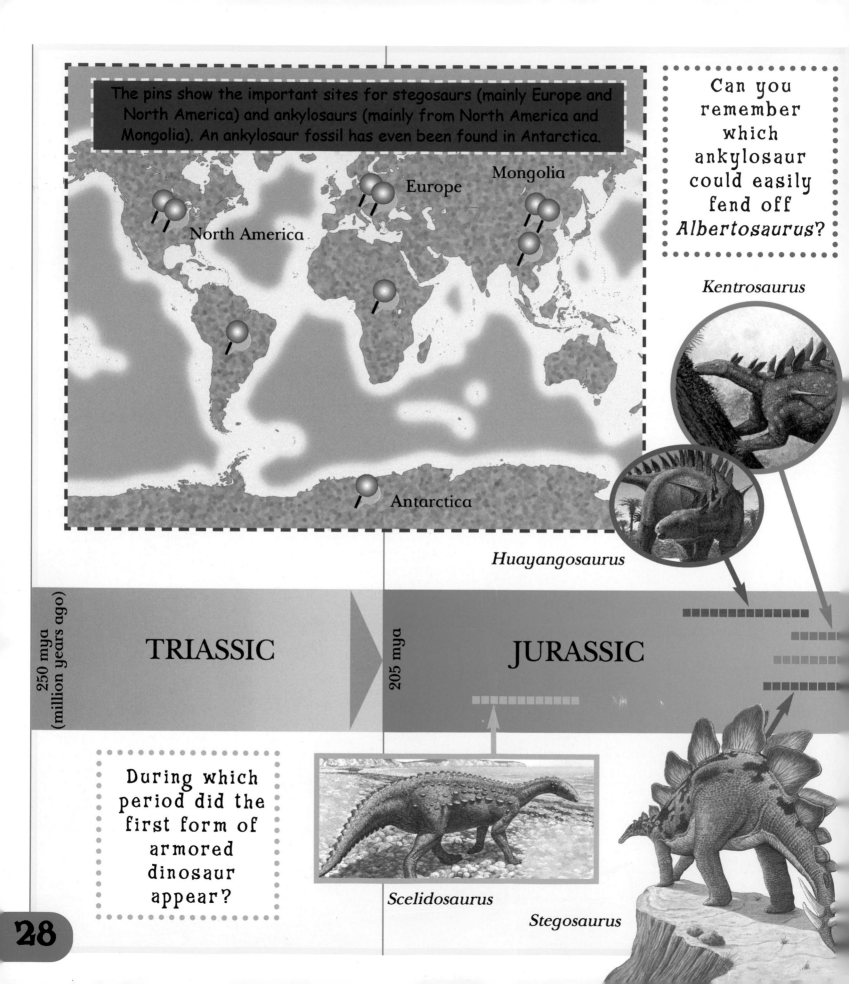

The pins show the important sites for stegosaurs (mainly Europe and North America) and ankylosaurs (mainly from North America and Mongolia). An ankylosaur fossil has even been found in Antarctica.

Europe

Mongolia

North America

Antarctica

Can you remember which ankylosaur could easily fend off *Albertosaurus*?

Kentrosaurus

Huayangosaurus

250 mya (million years ago)

TRIASSIC

205 mya

JURASSIC

During which period did the first form of armored dinosaur appear?

Scelidosaurus

Stegosaurus

Armored dinosaur world

The armored dinosaurs split into two groups in the Middle Jurassic—the plated stegosaurs and the bone-covered ankylosaurs. Stegosaurs were important in the Late Jurassic, ankylosaurs in the Late Cretaceous.

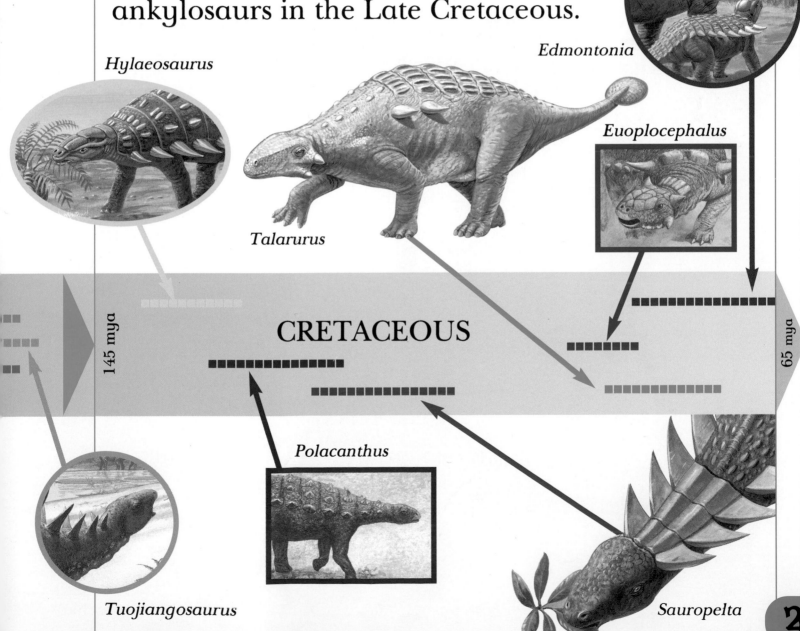

Hylaeosaurus

Edmontonia

Talarurus

Euoplocephalus

145 mya

CRETACEOUS

65 mya

Polacanthus

Tuojiangosaurus

Sauropelta

29

SAURISCHIA

THEROPODA

SAUROPODOMORPHA

ORNITHISCHIA

THYREOPHORA

MARGINOCEPHALIA

ORNITHOPODA

Dinosaur groups

There were five main groups of dinosaur: the armored plant eaters, called thyreophorans; the meat eaters, called theropods; the big, long-necked plant eaters, called sauropodomorphs; the horned dinosaurs, called marginocephalians; and the two-legged plant eaters, called ornithopods.

● *Sauropelta*

● *Diplodocus*

● *Tyrannosaurus rex*

● *Einosaurus*

● *Corythosaurus*

All dinosaurs are classed into one of two subgroups, the Saurischia and the Ornithischia, according to the arrangement of their three hip bones. The Saurischia, or "lizard hips," had the three hip bones all pointing in different directions. The Ornithischia, or "bird hips," had both of the lower hip bones running backward.

Hypsilophodon
(Ornithischia)

Carnotaurus
(Saurischia)

Glossary

Amphibian

A backboned animal that lives both in water and on land, such as a frog.

Ancestor

A historical forerunner of an animal group.

Ankylosaur

An armored plant-eating dinosaur, with a covering of bony plates and often a bony knob on the end of its tail.

Conifer

An evergreen tree, such as a pine, with cones and needles.

Continental drift

The movement of the continents over time.

Cretaceous

The geological period that lasted from 145 to 65 million years ago.

Deciduous tree

A tree that sheds its leaves.

Fossil

The remains of any ancient plant or animal, usually preserved in rock.

Geological

To do with the study of rocks.

Jurassic

The geological period that lasted from 205 to 145 million years ago.

Mesozoic

The geological era that lasted from 250 to 65 million years ago—the "age of dinosaurs."

Paleontologist

A person who studies fossils.

Predator

A meat eater—an animal that hunts others for food.

Radioactivity

"Rays" of chemical energy that are given off at fixed rates. Measuring radioactive elements in ancient rocks allows geologists to calculate the rocks' age.

Reptile

A backboned animal with scales, such as a dinosaur or a lizard. Most reptiles lay eggs and live on land.

Species

One particular kind of plant or animal, such as *Kentrosaurus* or the panda.

Stegosaur

A plant-eating dinosaur with bony plates and spines sticking upright along its back and tail.

Thyreophoran

An armored dinosaur, such as a stegosaur or ankylosaur.

Triassic

The geological period that lasted from 250 to 205 million years ago.

Vertebra (plural **Vertebrae**)

Together, the vertebrae make up the backbone. Each vertebra is like a cotton spool with bits sticking out for the ribs and muscles.

Index

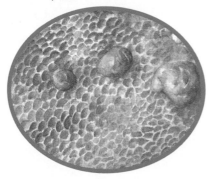